7-11-61

THE NATURAL DESIRE
FOR GOD

The Aquinas Lecture, 1948

The Natural Desire for God

Under the Auspices of the Aristotelian Society
of Marquette University

BY

THE REV. WILLIAM R. O'CONNOR

Professor of Dogmatic Theology
St. Joseph's Seminary
Dunwoodie, New York

MARQUETTE UNIVERSITY PRESS
MILWAUKEE, WISCONSIN
1948

Nihil Obstat

Gerard Smith, S.J., censor deputatus
Milwaukiae, die 3 mensis Septembris, 1948

Imprimatur

✠ Moyses E. Kiley
Archiepiscopus Milwaukiensis
Milwaukiae, die 17 mensis Septembris, 1948

PREFATORY

The Aristotelian Society of Marquette University each year invites a scholar to deliver a lecture in honor of St. Thomas Aquinas. Customarily delivered on the Sunday nearest March 7th, the feast day of the Society's patron saint, these lectures are called the Aquinas Lectures.

In 1948 the Society had the pleasure of recording the lecture of Reverend William R. O'Connor, S.T.L., Ph.D. It was delivered in the Marquette University High School Auditorium Sunday afternoon, March 7.

Father O'Connor was born in New York City in 1897. He attended the Cathedral College of that city before entering St. Joseph's Seminary, Dunwoodie, where he received his A.B. in 1920. Two years later, Father O'Connor was awarded the degree of S.T.L. at the North American College, University of Propaganda, Rome. He received his Ph.D. from Fordham University in 1943.

Father O'Connor was ordained on December 3, 1922. After returning to the United States he served as a curate at Monticello, New York in 1923, and then spent eight years at Liberty, New York, in the same capacity. He became professor of dogmatic theology at St. Joseph's Seminary, Dunwoodie, in 1931, where he is stationed at present. He was appointed prosynodal judge of the Archdiocese of New York in 1936 and in 1940 was made vice-official.

Father O'Connor is a member of the American Catholic Philosophical Association, the Catholic Biblical Association, and a director of the Catholic Theological society.

He is a contributor to the *Encyclopedia Britannica, Nelson's Encyclopedia, Ephemerides Theologicae Lovanienses, Thought, Theological Studies, The Jurist, The New Scholasticism, The American Ecclesiastical Review, The Homiletic and Pastoral Review, The Commonweal, The English Clergy Review, The Irish Ecclesiastical Record*. Besides contributing to scholarly journals and periodicals, Father O'Connor has published three books:

The Layman's Call, P. J. Kennedy and Sons, New York, 1942.

Sermon Outlines, Newman Bookshop, Westminster, Maryland, 1945.

The Eternal Quest, Longmans, Green & Co., New York, 1947.

To these the Aristotelian Society takes pleasure in adding *The Natural Desire for God.*

The Natural Desire for God

THE doctrine of a natural desire for God has had an interesting history. It is important, however, not to get off to a false start in telling the story. We may, if we choose, go back to the dawn of philosophy and seek the origin of the doctrine in the efforts men made to discover a principle or source to account for the universe. Invariably accompanying these efforts was a doctrine of a natural tendency in things to return to the source from which they came. Are we dealing here with a doctrine of a natural desire for God?

I

After *God and Philosophy* we must be cautious about using the term *God* to designate a first philosophical principle. It is Gilson's contention that the Greeks before Aristotle did not identify God with highest reality.[1] Water, air, fire, the indeterminate, may be first philosophical principles for the pre-Socratics, but they are not gods. The gods are "living powers, or forces, endowed with a will of their own, operating on human lives and swaying human destinies from above."[2] Greek gods are never inanimate; they are always living and immortal beings that are related more to man than to the world at large. A first cause or principle, on the other hand, is a "universally valid explanation for all that is, has ever been, or ever shall be."[3] No Greek before Aristotle ever thought of his God or gods in terms of such a principle.

This seems certainly to be the case with Plato, for whom highest reality lay in the realm of the forms, especially in the form of the Good. These forms, including the form of the Good, are not God; they are above the gods, and the form of the Good is even beyond being or essence.[4] The gods of Plato are not forms but souls, living divine souls that differ in degree but not in kind from human souls. Plato's God is not the form of the Good but a soul that perfectly imitates the forms.[5] As Demiurge he creates the world by putting order into pre-existing chaos.[6] Because he is a living being, he can serve as a model for other living beings to imitate, but he is not the ultimate goal of their striving. Occupying a midway position between the forms and the sensible world, Plato's God is in a much better position to act as a model for living and even non-living beings than the far-off, static forms. He himself participates in the forms by way of imitation and exhibits in himself a perfect copy for the sensible world to copy in its turn.[7]

We must not be misled by the wide use of the term *divine* in Plato, as in the Greeks generally, and see God as its equivalent wherever it is found. The divine for Plato is the self-existent, the eternal, the changeless, the immortal. It includes God and the gods, but it does not stop with them. It embraces the souls of heroes, the world-soul, even the world itself, the intellect, the forms, above all the form of the Good. There is a natural striving or desire in all things, animate and inanimate, to share in the forms, especially in the form of the Good, which is the teleological principle of all things.[8] Here is where we must exercise caution before we call this universal striving for the good in Plato a natural desire for God. The gods themselves are subject to the same natural law and necessity. Gilson's challenging statement still stands: "The identification of the Platonic Ideas with gods is still waiting for its historical justification."[9]

On their own level, then, which is beneath the level of highest reality, God and the gods may be said to be the objects of a natural striving on the part of the animate and inanimate world; but this is only a mediated striving on the way to the absolute objects of imitation, the forms. A theologian would liken it to the relative cult that is paid to statues and images; a cult that passes through these secondary objects to terminate in their prototypes, the persons who alone are capable of receiving absolute cult. It would be highly misleading to identify the Platonic imitation of God with the general finality of the good as the ultimate end of action, as we find it in the *Gorgias,* or as the object of universal desire, as in the *Philebus.* The Good and the forms are objects of imitation and participation as *ultimates,* while the striving to imitate God is not such a tendency towards an ultimate. The final end of all intelligent beings is not the vision of God but of the form of the Good. This is Plato's beatific vision for gods and men alike. In this fashion man becomes godlike, since he too can contemplate as God contemplates; but both God and man are contemplating the forms, and man becomes holy as God is holy through reverencing these divine objects of knowledge.[10]

Even the inanimate world imitates God to the extent that it strives to reproduce a likeness of him so far as this is possible. In fashioning the world the Demiurge formed it after the pattern of the eternal forms of which he himself is a perfect reflection. The world is constantly striving to fulfill the purpose of its maker by manifesting in itself the divine perfections after which it was modeled.[11] Because of this reflection of divine perfections the world is sometimes called a god.[12] At best, any natural striving for God in Plato is only a mediated imitation of the forms, above all of the form of the Good. Ultimate reality, lying as it does in the realm of the forms, alone constitutes the goal of universal natural desire.

What has been said of Plato of the fifth and fourth century B.C. can, we believe, be applied to Plotinus of the third century A.D. His doctrine of a natural desire for the One, which is also the Good, is often discussed in terms of a natural desire for God. This time it is Bréhier who warns us against too ready an identification of the One with God. Never, he tells us, do we find Plotinus calling the first principle God, except in a suspected text.[13] For Plotinus, a staunch defender of hellenistic polytheism, the gods were either souls that rule the world or stars. He is completely in the Platonic tradition when he locates the One not only above the gods, but beyond all the determinations that are found in every god—thought, life, being, and essence.[14]

Plotinus is as elastic as Plato in his use of the terms *divine* and *divinity,* but he exhibits the same reserve when there is question of applying the term *God* to the first philosophical principle. He tells us what it means to be a god: it means to be attached to the One.[15] If a god is a living being and if the One is beyond being and essence as well as life, clearly the One cannot be identified with God or any of the gods. Intelligence and the World-Soul, the second and third hypostases respectively, are gods: likewise the human soul and even the stars.[16] The first hypostasis, however, is beyond Intelligence and is unknowable, except in an ineffable mystical experience.[17] Because the One, which is also the Good, lies beyond knowledge and intelligence, it is possible for the natural desire for the Good to be independent of all cognition. This explains how souls are tending towards the Good even in sleep.[18] A theory of cascading descent from the One down to the sensible world has as its counterpart a natural striving, especially in souls, to rise to the level of the One and to be united with it in ecstatic contemplation. The One, or the Good, is the term of universal natural desire, but it is likewise misleading to speak of this as a natural desire for God. It is rather a striving for a principle that has no name. Plotinus himself assures us that all we can say about the One is that it is not anything.[19]

Proclus, it is true, identified the One with God through its identification with the Good.[20] This, however, occurred two centuries after Plotinus when Christian ideas had made their influence felt even in hostile pagan circles. The same identification was also made by the Christian neo-Platonist who goes under the name of Dionysius the Areopagite and who was clearly an admirer of Proclus. For him all things naturally desire the good, which is God, as their beginning, their cohesive power, and their end.[21] There is nothing remarkable about a Christian saying this; but the identification of God and the Good should not be anticipated, nor should a Christian mentality be imposed upon Plato or Plotinus.

An identification of God with the first philosophical principle was indeed made by Aristotle and, if we are to believe Gilson again, he was the first among the Greeks to do so.[22] Aristotle's prime mover, an immovable, separate substance, a pure act of thought eternally thinking on itself, is also his supreme God. This identification presents no difficulty because now we have a first philosophical principle that is a living, intelligent being and not something above thought and far removed even from the order of spiritual reality. In reference to this God there is in Aristotle a doctrine of natural desire, but in order to discover its nature we must first examine the nature of the God that is its goal.

Aristotle's God functions solely on the level of motion. An unmoved first mover is necessary in order to account for astronomical movements. There are, however, some forty-seven or fifty-five first movers, since "there must be substances which are of the same number as the movements of the stars, and in their nature eternal, and in themselves immovable, and without magnitude."[23] Clearly, then, Aristotle's first movers are first not in an absolute sense but only in a relative sense, since they are first only on the level of motion. Even on this level they do not function as efficient but as final causes, since they cause motion only as objects of love and desire.[24] These divine prime movers, in their intense self-concentration, are not even aware of the train of astral lovers following them around in eternal circular movement.

We have here a genuine doctrine of natural desire, for "upon such a principle [sc. a prime mover] depend the heavens and the world of nature."[25] Because the prime mover is also a God, we may call this a natural desire for God. It is, however, a natural desire for God only as a source of motion and not as the source and end of being. It may be questioned whether the notion of God is any more relevant in the philosophy of Aristotle than it is in the philosophies of Plato and of Plotinus, in spite of the advantage Aristotle's God enjoys in being identified with his first philosophical principle.

At the same time Aristotle has a well developed doctrine of natural desire. His teaching on the natural desire for God may not rise above the level of motion, but his teaching on natural desire in general is clear and understandable. In the *Physics* we learn what natural desire is: it is the tendency that originates in the natural form of every *ens naturae* as opposed to an artificial product, a tendency that constantly inclines such an *ens naturae* towards the end or purpose for which it exists.[26] Wherever a natural form is found, of the substantial or of the accidental order, a natural tendency or desire of this kind will also be found. It is found even in matter, and we can legitimately speak of the natural desire of matter for its connatural form.[27] St. Thomas Aquinas will tell us later that natural desire is an act not in the perfect sense of operation but in the imperfect sense of tendency, of inclination, of movement towards an operation that leads to a natural end, or to such an end itself. It is found in every nature and in every power of nature, but we are chiefly concerned with natural desire as it functions in the intellect and in the will.

The opening words of the *Metaphysics* give classical expression to the natural desire of the intellect: "All men by nature desire to know."[28] The intellect has by its nature or form a necessary tendency towards the acquisition of knowledge. For Aristotle this means the pursuit of truth in the present life, carried on according to the process of abstraction. Since the intellect is made to know, the more we know the more we are inclined to know. This tendency is what we mean by the natural desire of the intellect. The intellect never reaches a term, in Aristotle's view, beyond which there is nothing more to know. He has no certainty of personal immortality; and even if he had, he knows nothing about any object that could serve as a truly terminative end for the intellect, the knowledge of which would cause the natural desire for further knowledge to cease. Aristotle locates the end of man in the activity of his highest power, the intellect, speculating on the highest attainable truths. This activity is carried on without end in the present life and it results in philosophical wisdom which can serve as a normative or regulative end for man, since the philosopher will naturally organize his life according to wisdom. In living the life of a philosopher man is living a divine life, for he is acting according to a power within him that is divine, the intellect.[29] It is Aristotle's opinion that only in the achievement of philosophical wisdom is true happiness to be found.[30]

The will likewise, since it is a natural power, has its natural desire. The good is the end all men aim at,[31] and all agree that this good, common to all wills, is happiness.[32] While it is true that all men necessarily strive for happiness, this does not mean that they are tending of necessity towards any particular object as constituting their happiness. Men do not agree among themselves either as to the object that will yield true happiness or as to the activity in which it consists. Some locate it in pleasure, others in honor, others in wealth, others in health, others in virtue, others in practical wisdom, others in philosophical wisdom, others in external prosperity.[33] Aristotle himself identifies true happiness with the exercise of man's highest power, the intellect, speculating on the highest causes of being. Not all men know this, however, neither would all accept his conclusions if they did. This is why, for Aristotle, the human will has a necessary tendency towards happiness, but not towards any particular object or activity in which happiness may consist. He is perfectly consistent in saying, on the one hand, that philosophic wisdom produces happiness,[34] and, on the other, that there is no natural tendency to become a philosopher.[35] A philosopher locates the happy life in the pursuit of philosophical wisdom, but there is no natural necessity compelling him to do so.

II

What the Greeks could not do was done in a tradition where God means more than an unmoved first mover. It is not enough to identify God with the first philosophical principle to have a genuine natural desire for God in an unqualified sense of the term. The important point is to see in what sense this philosophical principle is first. Aristotle's God was first only in a relative sense, in the order of motion; and any natural desire for God he may have taught is confined to that order. In the Judaeo-Christian tradition God is first in an absolute sense: He is first in the order of being itself. All things have come from Him by way of creation and they tend towards Him to the extent that they are tending towards their own good or end. Every created good is a participation in and a likeness of the essential good that is God. In seeking their own good creatures are tending towards a likeness of the divine goodness; they are seeking to reproduce a divine perfection.[36] Here is a natural desire for God shared by all creation. It is, however, only an implicit desire that is involved in the explicit tendency of every creature towards the end for which it was made. No problem arises in a creationist philosophy over admitting this implicit desire for God in everything that owes its existence to His creative will.[37] Does this philosophy justify us in going further and asserting a formal, explicit tendency in every created intellectual nature towards God as its final end and beatitude?

It was inevitable that in the light of divine revelation men would no longer be content with Aristotle's views on the end of man. Revelation made known that man has a terminative end. "We shall see Him as He is"[38] is a statement of a fact and not of a mere possibility. Once it became known that the vision of God is man's beatitude, men longed and desired for a glimpse of this reward, exceeding great. For those who are in possession of this precious revelation, why should they, after the manner of pagans, speculate any further on the nature of human beatitude? The Fathers of the Church did not bring to this question a purely philosophical reason divorced from what they knew by revelation. They were not professional philosophers but religious teachers who were intent upon preserving and transmitting intact the deposit of faith. It is, I believe, in this light that we must judge a man like St. Augustine when he speaks of man's beatitude.

We shall look in vain in the writings of St. Augustine for a purely philosophical view of human nature, as we find it in Aristotle and, later, in St. Thomas Aquinas. The great African convert was much more concerned with the state in which man was created and born into this world than he was with his strictly essential constitution. Nature for him meant either the elevated state in which man began his career on earth or the fallen state in which he finds himself after sin.[39] Consequently, St. Augustine is uninterested in a purely natural end of man as Aristotle was, but he is deeply concerned with the only historical end man has ever had—the beatific vision of God.[40] He speaks as a psychologist and as a religious historian when he discusses man and his destiny, rather than as a strictly scientific philosopher or even theologian. This is why it is not easy to discover what St. Augustine thought of the purely natural tendencies of the soul, especially in reference to God, apart from their setting in fallen or redeemed man.

St. Augustine knew as well as Aristotle that man's will tends by a necessity of its nature towards happiness,[41] the notion of which is imprinted on our minds.[42] He also knew that true happiness or beatitude is found only in God. It is but a step to identify the happiness we are seeking by a necessity of our nature with God, and there does not seem to be any reason to doubt that St.

Augustine made this step.[48] Since God is in
fact the soul's beatitude, it is all one with him
to say that the soul is borne by its nature towards happiness and to say that it is borne by
its nature towards God. How he came to
make this identification is not a matter of
conjecture: he reveals it in three of his most
characteristic teachings.

In the first place, his doctrine of divine
illumination practically made the identification necessary. God is actually in the soul as
the truth that illumines the mind of every
man coming into this world. Beatitude, however, consists in the possession of the truth,
so that the soul is really tending towards God
when it is tending towards the truth that
beatifies. This is the theme of the *De beata
vita,* and it is a theme that will constantly recur
throughout the rest of his literary works. In
the *Confessions,* for instance, the search for
beatitude is the search for God. All men naturally seek to be happy; but they do not agree
as to what this happiness is, except to the extent that all are seeking the truth and wish to

rejoice in it. Because the truth that shines in every mind is identified with God, it is clear that all men in seeking a happy life in the pursuit of truth are seeking God.[44] God is there wherever truth is known; He is within every heart even though the heart wanders far from Him.[45] The soul may not know it, but it is seeking God when it is seeking its own happiness in the truth that all men naturally desire.[46] Even when we seek Him without, He is within, calling and crying and forcing open our deafness and chasing away our blindness.[47] God and the good itself, the notion of which is impressed on our minds as a standard of judging the good in this world, are interchangeable terms for St. Augustine; and the good that the soul is always seeking and cleaving to by love is nothing else than God.[48]

Secondly, the natural image of God in the soul also furnishes a foundation for a natural tendency towards Him whose image is there. The mind always remembers, knows, and loves itself; and this threefold power is for

St. Augustine a natural image of the Trinity.[49]
Considered in itself, before it becomes a par-
taker of God, the mind always bears this
image of Him, so that through it the soul is
capable of God and able to partake of Him.
The image may be worn out, obscured, or
defaced, but it is always there. It lies beneath
the holiness and justice in which man was
created and which are lost by sin. The loss of
sanctifying grace defaces and tarnishes the
image of God in the mind, but does not
entirely remove it. When man is renewed
again in justice, the natural image is repaired
and restored.[50] At this point St. Augustine
makes an important distinction between *knowing* and *considering.* The soul always knows
itself and God through His image, but it does
not always consider what it knows. The
knowledge the soul has of itself as made in
the image of God is stored up in memory
even while we are actually thinking of something else.[51] This is why the soul is always
capable of God whether it is actually aware
of Him or not. Even in sin the soul bears this

natural likeness to the supreme good, and sinners strive after nothing else than some kind of likeness to God.[52]

Thirdly, St. Augustine's doctrine of the natural weight of the will implies a natural desire for God. The will holds the primacy among man's powers. This is evident from the fact that preceding every act of knowledge is an act of will, an appetite or desire to know.[53] In the *Physics* of Aristotle we read that every body is borne by its natural weight towards a determined place in the universe, where it finds its repose. This is called its natural place. In seeking its natural place fire is borne upwards and a stone downwards. In a somewhat similar fashion St. Augustine conceives man and his will. In each soul, as in each body, is a weight which pulls and inclines it constantly towards its natural place, where it too will find its repose. This weight is the soul's natural love, and it is this that moves the will instinctively: "My weight is my love; by it I am borne whithersoever I am borne."[54] God, however, is charity, and charity is love, and love is the internal weight that belongs to the nature of the will. This doctrine of the natural weight of the will, as Gilson remarks, puts God at the very center of the soul.[55] It gives meaning to the teaching of the *Soliloquies* that every being capable of loving is loving God whether he is aware of it or not.[56]

In the light of these principles we can understand St. Augustine when he speaks of a hunger of the soul that corresponds to bodily hunger;[57] it is a hunger for happiness,[58] and whoever possesses God is happy.[59] The steady presence of God in the soul makes men happy;[60] and the soul dies when God leaves it, when it lacks a blessed life, just as the body dies when the soul leaves it.[61] Since God is the common good of men and of angels, since He is their beatific good, it belongs to their nature to cleave to God, so that every vice is an injury to nature.[62] The natural desire for God as our beatitude gives meaning to the statement: "It is the especial wretchedness of man not to be with Him, without whom he cannot be."[63] This doctrine finds its most eloquent expression in the moving sentence of the *Confessions*: "Thou hast formed us for thyself, and our hearts are restless until they find rest in thee."[64]

How much of this teaching is Christian contemplative wisdom and how much is pure philosophy may be hard to determine with accuracy. What emerges, however, is that St. Augustine placed, or rather discovered, in the soul of every man, prior to grace and prior even to conscious reflection, a natural desire for God as our beatitude. This identification is even more basic in Augustinianism than the doctrine of divine illumination. It is true, so long as the divine illumination of truth was retained in the Augustinian tradition, a natural desire for God followed upon it as a necessary consequence. We see this in the teaching of St. Bonaventure, a pure Augustinian, for whom the soul has an innate knowledge of the existence of God as its supreme good, since it is made in His image and likeness. This gives rise to a natural desire for God as our beatitude: "The soul naturally tends towards the one in whose image it has been made, in order that in Him it may be beatified."[65]

A time came, however, when Augustinianism dropped the doctrine of divine illumination and caught up with the doctrine of abstraction. Did this mean the abandonment of the natural desire for God as our beatitude? By no means. John Duns Scotus found no difficulty in relinquishing the former but retaining the latter. Reverting to an older Plotinian conception of a natural tendency of the will towards the good that is independent of cognition, he affirmed the existence of a natural, necessary tendency in every created will towards happiness in particular. Happiness in particular is not happiness in general, which is happiness in the abstract following cognition. Happiness in particular is an object which alone can adequately fulfill the cravings of the will, and this object is God. The will is set by its nature towards the vision of God as the supreme beatitude and final end of man.[66] This innate, natural tendency has nothing to do with cognition; it is prior to actual knowledge and it consists in a fundamental relation to God that persists even in sleep. Divine illumination may go, but this radical ordination of the will towards God as man's beatitude remains as the core of authentic Augustinianism.

III

Here is where St. Thomas Aquinas made a great refusal. He was well aware of the so-called Augustinian or historical use of the terms *nature* and *natural*.[67] He was, however, a scientific philosopher and theologian as well as a deeply religious thinker, and as such he could distinguish a proper from an improper sense of these terms where St. Augustine did not. As a Christian theologian, viewing human nature and the end of man in their factual, historical perspectives, he had every inducement to remain in the Augustinian tradition and make the same identification that St. Augustine made. Is it not true that

God is our beatitude? Has it not been re-
vealed that the vision of God is the end of
man? That is the whole point. It is a re-
vealed truth that the vision of God is the
only historical end man has ever had, so that
the purely natural man with a purely natural
end has never existed. Does this mean that
the human will by its very nature has an
innate, necessary tendency towards God, or
the vision of God, as our beatitude? Does it
mean that the intellect is tending by its nature
as intellect, prior to all actual knowledge,
towards this vision as the only object that can
finally put an end to its unlimited craving
for truth? In other words, has every intellectual creature a natural desire for the beatific
vision? When the question is worded in this
fashion St. Thomas' answer is, I believe, a
straightforward no.

The cardinal principle that guides him in
this matter is the primacy of intellect over
will. This means a primacy of intellect over
even the innate, natural tendency of the will
towards its end, which we call its natural

desire. The will depends by its nature upon the intellect; it owes its origin to it, and it always remains rooted in intelligence. By definition the will is the rational or intellectual appetite, for it is the appetite of the soul that follows an apprehended good.[68] Each power of the soul has its own good or end, which in the case of the will is happiness.[69] The necessary striving of the will towards happiness is its natural desire. The happiness, however, that constitutes the end of the will is not independent of cognition. The notion of happiness must first be present in the intellect before there can be any natural tendency of the will in its direction. All men know what happiness in general means.[70] A knowledge of this kind is involved in the understanding of first principles; it is not something men have to reason to as a conclusion that flows from premisses.[71] The will naturally desires not only happiness in general but all that is seen to have a necessary connection with happiness, such as the knowledge of truth (which is properly a function

of intellect), continuation in life, and per-
sistence in being.[72]

At this point St. Thomas makes the simple
avowal that no one during the course of a
normal existence on earth ever comes face to
face with an object that measures up to all
the requirements of the good, apart from
this general notion of happiness. This is
true even in the case of God as He is known
to us here. For this reason man's will is necessarily striving for happiness, but it is not
tending of necessity towards any particular
object as identified with this happiness.[73]

This principle enables us to see where St.
Thomas differs from St. Augustine in his
teaching on the natural desire for God.
Whether divine illumination may be called
a form of knowledge or not, St. Augustine
taught that even in this life the mind sees
or makes an identification of God with man's
beatitude, so that the will cannot help being
drawn towards Him by natural necessity. For
St. Thomas we do not see in this life an
identification of God with the good in gen-

eral or with happiness. For this reason the human will is not drawn by natural necessity towards God or the vision of God as the object that constitutes our beatitude. The knowledge of God we have in this life is indirect, mediate, abstract, obscure. It does not present God to us as He really is. If an object appeared to us as good from every point of view, the will would of necessity tend towards it and seek its rest in it. This will be the case in the next life when we shall see God as He is, but we do not see Him now. We know from revelation that He is our true beatitude and ultimate end and we should freely adhere to Him, even though we cannot do so by natural necessity. The mere fact that we are capable of turning away from God as our ultimate end proves that we have not a determined tendency towards Him as our beatitude as we have towards happiness in general.

We may, it is true, conclude by a necessary chain of reasoning that God alone can satisfy the cravings of the human heart for happiness and of the created intellect for truth.

Reasoning, however, even though it is con-
clusive, does not present God to us; it does
not make Him appear as He really is. To
assent of necessity to the truth of a proposi-
tion is one thing; to tend of necessity towards
an object seen as fulfilling all the requirements of the good is another. In fact, we
know that all men do not accept the revelation that God has made concerning our
destiny, nor do all accept the chain of reasoning that leads to the identification of God
with our highest good. They necessarily desire happiness, but they do not necessarily
desire God as their happiness. St. Thomas
fully agrees with Aristotle that only happiness, or the good in general, exercises a necessary compulsion upon the will in the present
life.[74]

Yet St. Thomas admits that God is involved in the natural desire for happiness,
since He is in fact our beatitude. This does
not mean, he immediately adds, that we recognize God formally and explicitly in the
happiness that we are seeking by a necessity

of nature. Man naturally desires happiness, and what is naturally desired must be naturally known by him. Only in a confused way, however, does this natural knowledge of happiness that precedes its natural desire imply a knowledge of the existence of God, or of the fact that He is our beatitude. We see a person approaching in the distance and we do not recognize him as Mr. X, although he will turn out to be Mr. X on closer inspection. In a similar way the happiness we are all seeking by a necessity of our nature is not recognized by us as identified with God who is in truth our highest good.[75] This is evident from the fact that so many people locate the perfect good they are seeking in riches, in pleasures, or in something else, and not in God.[76] The same implicit tendency towards God is found in the natural appetite all things have for their proper perfections, to the extent that these perfections are likenesses of the divine perfection. This too is only an implicit desire for God that is present in every creature, and it does not imply an explicit tendency or desire for God as our beatitude.[77]

Are we to conclude, then, that for St. Thomas Aquinas there is no natural desire for God in this life, beyond the implicit desire that is contained in every tendency towards the good? No, for he has a doctrine of a genuine natural desire for God; only it is not to be conceived in terms of the will tending of necessity towards God as our beatitude, nor in terms of the intellect tending by its nature towards the vision of God as its connatural end.

Every power, every nature, has its natural tendency, which is its natural desire. In the intellect is a tendency flowing from its natural form as intellect towards knowledge and truth. "All men by nature desire to know," said Aristotle, and St. Thomas gives us a special application of this general principle in his doctrine of a natural desire for the vision of God. Once we know that God exists, the intellect is still unsatisfied; it tends by its very nature towards a further knowledge of Him. We know that God exists through the celebrated five ways: does anyone imagine that the human mind is completely satisfied when it reaches the end of the five ways? The intellect cannot be satisfied with partial truth or incomplete knowledge; it tends by a necessity of its nature to know the essence of any object once it knows this much about it, that it exists. The natural curiosity that has been aroused by a knowledge of the existence of God will not and cannot be stilled short of an intellectual vision of Him that will put an end to all further cravings for knowledge in this direction.[78] While this desire is formally a tendency of the intellect, it may be said to belong to the will only to the extent that the will naturally desires not only its own good, which is happiness, but as a consequence the good of all our powers and of the whole man. Since truth is the good of the intellect, the will naturally desires that the intellect advance from *an sit* to *quid sit* cognition, particularly in regard to anything whose existence alone is known.[79]

It is important, however, to see that to desire to know an object is not the same as desiring an object already known. The intellect naturally desires to know more about God once it knows that He exists; but this does not mean that the will of man naturally desires God as our beatitude before He is seen as He is in Himself. Because the latter is impossible, it is a matter of indifference to us in the present life whether the object whose existence is known happens to be our true ultimate end and beatitude, so far as the natural tendency to know more about it is concerned. Even in a state of pure nature, where the vision of God would not have been granted as the end of man, the natural desire to see Him would still be present after His existence came to be known by reason alone.[80]

The presence of this natural desire, whose point of departure is the knowledge that God exists, does not imply that it must be satisfied, nor does it mean that the vision of God is the natural end of the created intellect. To have an inexhaustible craving for knowledge and truth is natural; to have this craving satisfied completely and finally is not natural but supernatural. The only conclusion St. Thomas draws from the presence of the natural desire to see God in every intellectual creature is that the vision of God is possible; but he expressly denies its connaturality.[81] Once a thing is known to exist, it is possible to know what it is; even though this possibility cannot be realized naturally.[82] A heavenly body was once known to exist by mathematical calculations long before it was actually seen. The fact that it was known to exist meant that it was possible to see it, but it did not mean that it was possible to see it with the naked eye. A telescope was necessary to realize this possibility. Likewise in regard to God: we can and do know with certitude that He exists. Besides, God in Himself is supremely intelligible and eminently knowable. If He is not known as He is in Himself, the defect always lies not with Him but with the created intellect.[83] This leads to the all-important question: what is the natural end of the created intellect?

For St. Thomas Aquinas no created intellect tends by its nature towards a direct and immediate vision of God as its natural end. The analogy of being makes this impossible. Knowledge always takes place according to the way in which the knowing subject exists. Where the mode of being of an object altogether transcends the mode of being of the knower, a direct knowledge of the essence of such an object is above the nature of the knower. God's mode of being is, as it were, to be subsisting being; every creature, spiritual or material, is not subsisting being but a compound of essence and existence. This fact alone makes it impossible for the divine substance to be the natural end of any created intelligence.[84]

This does not exclude a knowledge of God from the natural end of the created intellect. St. Thomas teaches that the ultimate end of an intellectual nature is to know God in some way or other *(quoquo modo),* and

that however little we know of God will serve
as the ultimate end of the intellect far better
than a perfect knowledge of inferior things.[85]
The *natural* capacity of the intellect, he tells
us, extends to a knowledge of all genera and
species and the order of things.[86] God as
reflected in creatures is at the summit of the
natural knowledge of the intellect, but not
God as He is in Himself. The fact that the
vision of God will put an end to the unlimited
cravings of the intellect for truth does not
make this vision the natural end of man. To
see the substance of God, St. Thomas repeats,
transcends the limits of every created nature,
since it belongs to a created intelligence to
know only according to its mode of being.[87]

The composite mode of being of the
created intellect constitutes an impediment or
a defect which makes the vision of God not
only naturally unattainable but in no way our
natural end. St. Thomas refers to it as the
impediment of the inferiority of our nature,
and it is removed by the supernatural elevation of grace in the present life and the light

of glory in the next. The removal of the impediment enables the natural desire to see God to come to fruition; but, in the present case, due to the nature of the object and to the nature of the intellect that seeks to know it, the term of the natural desire is not the natural end of the intellect. A natural desire would be altogether in vain if, after the removal of the impediment, it were still impossible to reach its term.[88]

IV

This teaching of St. Thomas Aquinas broke with a long tradition. Almost immediately, however, the tradition closed in again in the person of John Duns Scotus, and the terms in which he stated the problem have lasted down to the present day.

Duns Scotus could not differ from St. Thomas on a more radical issue than he did in this whole question. Since for Scotus every intellect is open to all being, it must have all being, taken in a univocal sense, for its object. This means that God is the principal and primary object of every intellect. No created intellect can rest content in any substance or being short of the highest and best, so that every intellectual creature, angelic or human, is ordered to God as its end.[89] Because the will naturally tends towards the good of all our powers, it follows that the human will has a natural appetite for beatitude not in general but in particular, which means the vision of the highest being, God.[90] In this fashion John Duns Scotus restated the question in terms of the will striving of necessity towards God as its beatitude, instead of in terms of the intellect striving by its nature towards a knowledge of the essence of God after His existence is already known, as St. Thomas had done. From this time on the problem will be stated as Duns Scotus stated it, even by those who differ from him and who would like to defend the view of St. Thomas but who are puzzled as to what he meant by his celebrated doctrine of a natural desire for the "beatific" vision.

In the view of Duns Scotus and conse-
quent upon his univocal concept of being,
the will necessarily, perpetually, and in the
highest degree is tending towards the vision
of God as the final end and ultimate beatitude
of man. This natural striving is altogether
independent of previous cognition. It results
from the nature of intellect and from the
nature of will. The intellect is an open door
to all being, including God as He is in Himself; and what is more natural for an open
door than to be closed? The closing of this
door by the vision of God, the supreme being, is the natural end of man. It is only the
accident of our present state that the essences
of material things are for the time being the
proper object of the human intellect. This is
not due to the nature of the intellect but it is
an arrangement of the will of God either
as a punishment for original sin or as a means
of uniting the operations of sense and intellect in the present life. Neither the sep-
arated soul after death nor the soul in the
risen body will suffer this impediment to its

natural tendency towards the vision of God as the natural end and beatitude of man.[91]

The principle of the open door has proved very attractive since the days of Duns Scotus. Not a few even interpret St. Thomas' teaching in this Scotistic sense. Dominic Soto, a sixteenth century Dominican, completely adopts the position of Duns Scotus. Man is made in the image and likeness of God. This means not only a natural capacity for seeing God but even a natural inclination towards this end. In the will is an innate, natural tendency, a *pondus naturae,* towards the vision of God as the supreme beatitude and ultimate end of man.[92]

Our century is witnessing a resurgence of the Augustinian-Scotistic position that dates back to the teaching of Sestili on the natural desire to see God implicitly contained in man's natural desire for complete and perfect beatitude.[93] It received fresh impetus from Rousselot's doctrine that intelligence is the faculty of the real only because it is the faculty of the divine.[94] It gathered momentum with the teaching of De Broglie, similar to that of Sestili, on the natural desire for the beatific vision implicitly contained in the intellect's search for truth and in the natural tendency of the will towards beatitude.[95] Maréchal's view is the same: in man is a metaphysical tendency towards the beatific vision that requires elevation and grace for its fulfilment, but which is basically a tendency towards a perfection that cannot be attained by his purely natural powers.[96] With Dom Laporta this basic tendency of our nature becomes a transcendental ordination of finality towards the beatific vision as the end of man. This ordination of his nature is not an elicited act that is either necessary or free, for then it would depend upon cognition. It is rather an ontological natural appetite of the will, independent of cognition, towards the beatific vision as the supernatural beatitude of an intellectual creature.[97] O'Mahony teaches the same.[98]

What may be called the Augustinian-Scotistic movement has reached its climax today in a work of great power and charm. I refer to Father de Lubac's *Surnaturel*.[99] The author sees no break in continuity in the essential positions taken by St. Augustine, St. Bonaventure, St. Thomas Aquinas, Duns Scotus, and Dominic Soto on this question of the end of man. Their essential agreement, he tells us, lies in this: no spiritual nature, human or angelic, can have any other end except the beatific vision of God. A state of pure nature, with a purely natural end short of the beatific vision, is inconceivable and impossible for an intellectual nature made in the image of God. In such a nature is an absolute, unconditional, though inefficacious, tendency towards this supernatural end. There is thus no break in continuity between the natural and the supernatural; for the latter is not added to, or superimposed on, the former, but is rather its only possible complement and perfection.[100]

Does this mean an exigency in a created spiritual nature for the beatific vision? Father de Lubac does not like this word, and in rendering it "innocent" he shows great originality. If we conceive the spirit of man along Aristotelian lines, cut off from its relation to its creator, with exigency meaning something strictly due to such a nature, there is no exigency in this sense for the supernatural. If, however, with the Fathers of the Church we conceive of a spiritual creature as always depending upon the Creator by its nature and bearing His image, then we may speak of an exigency in such a creature for its creator as its end. God is completely free to give the gift of an intellectual nature, the image of His own. He would never have given it, however, unless He were prepared, so to speak, to give another gift as its connatural complement, the beatific vision, in which alone can be found the fulfilment of the inexhaustible cravings of a spiritual creature for truth and beatitude. The natural desire for the beatific vision is God's own will embedded in such a creature; and when God answers this appeal, He is replying to His own will. From the standpoint of God we see the absolute and unconditional character of this appeal, while from the standpoint of the created intelligence we see clearly how inefficacious are the forces of unaided nature before an end that is supernatural.[101]

V

A radical opposition exists between St. Augustine and Duns Scotus on the one hand and St. Thomas Aquinas on the other over the fundamental point at issue here. St. Thomas is just as much an advocate of the open door of the intellect as Duns Scotus, since its object, he tells us, is all being—*ens universale*.[102] It makes a difference, however, how being is understood when we wish to discover how all being can be the object of a created intellect. If it is understood univocally, as Duns Scotus understood it, then we can at least understand why he taught that the divine essence itself, and as it exists in itself, comes within the natural range of the created intellect. The need of the *lumen gloriae* in this view becomes purely extrinsic; it is needed merely to take the place of created species which have no part to play in the beatific vision. This "light," however, is not absolutely indispensable, and it does not give to the intellect a capacity for an end it did not have before.[103]

If, on the other hand, being is understood analogously, as St. Thomas understands it, then it is impossible for an object that is absolutely uncomposed in its mode of being to become, while remaining in that mode of being, the natural end of a power that is composed in its mode of being. This object must, as it were, be brought down to the level of the knowing power before it can become naturally known or knowable. It will be natural for the soul after death to know other separate substances such as angels, since they like the intellect that knows them are spirits whose being is composed; but it will never be natural for any created spirit to know the self-subsisting Being as it is in itself. This Being cannot be naturally known, except as it is reflected in creatures.[104]

It follows that a state of pure nature, with a purely natural end, is conceivable and possible. The univocal notion of being compels Duns Scotus to regard the closing of the door as part of the nature of the intellect. The analogical notion of being, held by St. Thomas Aquinas, sees no natural necessity in an open door to be closed, at least if we are speaking of the open door of the created intellect. This door was not made to be closed, so far as its nature is concerned. It will always remain open until it meets the first truth, which is all truth; but in its natural state the intellect not only will not but cannot meet this truth, as it were, face to face; and it was never made to do so. All that it learns of God, either in the present life or in the next, no matter how high and satisfying this knowledge may be, will not be definitive; it will always leave room for more. The capacity of the intellect for truth can never be filled naturally, and this condition belongs to the nature of a spiritual creature.[105]

It is purely an assumption that the natural end of man must be a terminative end, completely and perfectly satisfying his natural cravings for truth and for happiness on the natural plane. Aristotle discovered the natural end of man, and it is not a terminative end but an end only in a normative and regulative sense. Aristotle, it is true, confined his consideration to the present life; but St. Thomas Aquinas, aware of the immortality of the whole soul, accepts his essential position even for the future life, when he asserts that perfect happiness will never be found by man or angel in their natural condition. Natural ultimate happiness is one thing; it is not perfect beatitude. Above this is another happiness, which alone is happiness *simpliciter* and perfect beatitude. This, however, consists in the vision of God, which is not the natural but the supernatural end of man.[106]

From the standpoint of its nature a created spirit, angelic or human, was never made to reach an ultimate term in its eternal quest for truth and consequently for happiness, be-

yond which it could not go because its natural
desires would be completely satisfied. The
very completeness and perfection of the non-
discursive, non-abstractive, intuitional and in-
fused knowledge of the angels only leaves
them with a greater void and a more vehe-
ment natural desire to dispel their ignorance
and to see face to face that infinite Substance
which they know exists but which they also
know lies far beyond their natural capacity
to attain. They know better than we that the
vision of God is not their natural end; yet
their natural desire to see God is more intense than ours in proportion to the greater
clarity and directness of their grasp of the
truth of His existence and of His attributes
as they are reflected in the spirit world.[107] I
could agree with Father de Lubac that a state
of pure nature is impossible for a spiritual
creature if it were true that the natural end
of such a creature, like the supernatural end,
had to be a terminative end. This, however,
in my opinion is an unproved assumption.
Because faith and theology teach the genuine-

ly terminative character of the supernatural end of man, it does not follow that a purely natural end must also have the same characteristic. De Lubac's whole view is professedly more the fruit of a theological outlook on man and his destiny than the result of purely rational speculation. It may seem to be in harmony with the Christian wisdom that dominates the speculations of St. Augustine, although even here great reserve is needed in order to safeguard properly the gratuitousness of the supernatural. I do not think, however, that it harmonizes equally well with the philosophical wisdom St. Thomas Aquinas has taught us to respect.

The influence of John Duns Scotus has made itself felt even among those who reject his natural ordination to supernatural beatitude. They wish to defend St. Thomas' view, but it leaves them puzzled because they cannot understand how there can be a natural tendency in the created will towards the beatific vision. Having stated the problem as Duns Scotus states it, in terms of the will tending

towards its beatitude, they do not know what
to make of it. We are faced with the phe-
nomenon of no common agreement among
the interpreters of St. Thomas from the days
of the great commentators down to the present as to what this natural desire really means.
Bañez solves the difficulty by reducing the
desire in question to non-repugnance, suit-
ableness, and obediential capacity.[108] Cajetan
would do the same, only he thinks that St.
Thomas was speaking as a theologian and
not as a philosopher, and as such he was referring to a desire to see God that naturally
arises after we behold His supernatural effects. This desire may also be called natural
simply because our nature is its subject.[109]

Cajetan's view is opposed by Sylvester of
Ferrara, who clearly saw that St. Thomas was
not speaking about a natural desire for supernatural beatitude, but only for a vision of
God as the first cause of natural phenomena
visible in the universe. Sylvester of Ferrara,
in my opinion, was on the right track and he
would have seen the exact teaching of St.

Thomas if he had not stated the problem in terms of the will, as Duns Scotus had done, instead of in terms of the intellect, with St. Thomas himself. For him St. Thomas' natural desire to see the divine essence is an act of the will that is necessarily elicited following upon a knowledge of the existence of God. This act is necessary, however, only in regard to its specification; it is not necessary in regard to its exercise.[110]

St. Thomas, we must remember, has a doctrine of the will enjoying freedom of exercise but not of specification before the good or happiness in general. We are free to act or not in regard to this object; yet, if we choose to act, the act must be one of acceptance; it cannot be one of rejection. Sylvester of Ferrara transfers this distinction to the natural desire for the vision of God. In doing so he shows that in his view the vision of God stands in the same relation to the will, even in this life, that the good or happiness in general does for St. Thomas. Since this good, the vision of God, appears

before the will as good from every point of
view, we are free to elicit or not to elicit an
act in regard to it; but, if we choose to act
at all, the act must be one of desire for this
vision; it cannot be one of rejection.[111]

At this point Sylvester of Ferrara shows
that, all unwittingly, he belongs to the Scotistic rather than to the Thomistic family, at
least on this question of the natural desire
for God. For St. Thomas, as we have seen,
no object, not even God as He appears to us
here, or the vision of God as we understand
it now, is seen as good from every point of
view. This is the reason why many reject God
or the vision of God as their beatitude.[112]
The freedom we enjoy in regard to eliciting
an act of desire to see God as the first cause
of natural effects is a freedom both of specification and of exercise. In denying this, Sylvester of Ferrara simply goes against human
experience. His teaching reveals the futility
of hoping to arrive at a satisfactory solution
of St. Thomas' doctrine of a natural desire for
the vision of God, if it is discussed solely in

terms of the will and its tendency towards
beatitude.

The so-called four great commentators on
this question—Bañez, Cajetan, Dominic Soto,
and Sylvester of Ferrara—have set the pattern
for all subsequent interpretations. Where
they do not formally and explicitly adopt the
teaching of Duns Scotus, as Dominic Soto did,
they at least allow Duns Scotus to state the
problem for them. In doing so the commentators cross and confuse two natural desires
that St. Thomas himself kept distinct: the
natural desire of the intellect for knowledge
and the natural desire of the will for happiness. Because the will of man in this life
tends of necessity and by its nature towards
no particular object as identified with his
beatitude, not even God, St. Thomas never
speaks of a natural desire for the "beatific"
vision. Those who speak this way imply the
existence of a natural tendency in the will
towards the vision of God as our beatitude.
For St. Thomas the natural desire for God is
the natural tendency of the intellect for a

knowledge of God that cannot be satisfied short of a direct vision of Him, once we know that He exists. This does not make the vision of God the natural end of the intellect, for to have an inexhaustible craving for truth is part and parcel of the nature of a spiritual creature. It is important, too, to keep in mind that the natural desire for the vision of God that St. Thomas teaches does not begin to function except on the hypothesis that the existence of God is already known.

Seen against the background of history, St. Thomas' teaching on the natural desire for God was only an interlude in the Augustinian-Scotistic tradition. Those who continue to speak of his doctrine of a natural desire for the "beatific" vision bear witness to the living influence of that tradition today. While he cannot be fitted into the chain that links up St. Augustine, St. Bonaventure, Duns Scotus, and Dominic Soto on this question, yet his position is no less Christian than that of the tradition with which he broke. His position, however, will continue to appear incoherent and even contradictory, so long as it is stated in terms of that tradition instead of in his own.

NOTES

1. Étienne Gilson, *God and Philosophy*, New Haven, Yale University Press, 1941, ch. 1.

2. *Ibid.*, 7-8.

3. *Ibid.*, 20.

4. "ἐπέκεινα τῆς οὐσίας," *Republic*, 509.

5. This is much debated matter, but the evidence seems to be definitely against the identification of Plato's God with the form of the Good. For a summary of the arguments and authorities on both sides see Culbert Gerow Rutenber, *The Doctrine of the Imitation of God in Plato*, New York, King's Crown Press, 1946, 4-17. The absence of any reference to Gilson's *God and Philosophy* in this dissertation is surprising. For Rutenber "Plato's God was the divine soul whose mind completely grasps the whole realm of forms" (102).

6. *Timaeus*, 30a.

7. This theme is well developed in Rutenber's work.

8. Cf. Rutenber, 62.

9. *God and Philosophy*, 27.

10. *Theaetetus*, 176. Cf. Rutenber, 79.

11. *Timaeus*, 29-30.

12. *Timaeus,* 34b; 92c.

13. "Plotin ne prononce jamais le nom de Dieu (sauf dans un texte suspect) à propos du premier principe: ce nom ne revient fréquemment dans ses écrits qu'à propos des âmes rectrices du monde ou des astres qui, seules, sont proprement pour lui des dieux et à propos desquels il défend le polythéisme hellenique" — Émile Bréhier, *Histoire de la philosophie,* Paris, Alcan, 1926-34, I, 459. Cf. William Ralph Inge, *The Philosophy of Plotinus,* 2 vols., London, Longmans, Green and Co., 1923; II, 82, n. 3: "Plotinus occasionally calls the One θεός, e.g. in I, 1, 8; but those modern critics who habitually speak of the Neoplatonic Absolute as 'God' only mislead their readers." A reference to Bréhier's edition of the *Enneads* (*Plotin, Ennéades,* Budé Collection, Paris, 1931, I, 44, 11, ll. 8-10) will reveal that the text in which the term God appears to be applied the first principle is not free from corruption. It is curious, too, to see how Inge does not always follow his own advice. From the standpoint of pagan Greek theology the Good of Plato and the One of Plotinus could be gods only in a metaphorical sense.

14. The complete transcendence of the One is well seen in *Enneads,* V, 4, *1*; V, 3, *13-14*; V, 5, *6, 8-11.*

15. *Enneads,* VI, 9, 8: "θεὸς γὰρ τὸ ἐκείνῳ [*sc.* τῷ ἑνὶ] συνημμένον." Dodds tells us that Plotinus applies the term *God* not only to νοῦς and the

universal soul, but also to the human soul and to the stars. In the Plotinian use of the term it chiefly covers the whole of the second hypostasis (E. R. Dodds, *Proclus, the Elements of Theology,* Oxford, 1933, 268).

16. Cf. *Enneads,* IV, 8, 5; VI, 9, 9; V, 1, 4.

17. *Enneads,* VI, 9, 4; VI, 7, 36. Dodds, *op. cit.,* p. 311, tells us that the One of Plotinus is unknowable except in a mystical union that does not yield any communicable knowledge.

18. *Enneads,* V, 5, 12.

19. *Enneads,* V, 3, 13. For Inge, *op. cit.,* I, 160-1, the goal of Plotinus' mysticism is a state and not a person; union with the One does not mean a personal union between a personal God and man. Cf. also D. J. Leahy, *St. Augustine on Eternal Life,* London, Burns, Oates, 1939, 19.

20. *The Elements of Theology,* 113; Dodds, 101.

21. *The Divine Names,* IV, 4 (cf. C. E. Rolt, *Dionysius the Areopagite on the Divine Names and the Mystical Theology,* Translations of Christian Literature, series I, Greek texts, *S. P. C. K.,* London, Macmillan, 1940, 90-94).

22. *God and Philosophy,* 32.

23. *Metaphysics,* 1073a37; cf. 1072a. A convenient text for English readers is *The Student's Oxford Aristotle,* translated under the editorship of W. D. Ross, Oxford, 1942, Vol. IV.

24. *Metaphysics,* 1072a25-1072b5.

25. *Metaphysics,* 1072b14.

26. *Physics,* 192b; 255b. The *Physics* are in Vol. II of *The Student's Oxford Aristotle.*

27. *Physics,* 192a20-25.

28. *Metaphysics,* 980a.

29. *Ethica Nicomachea,* 1177b30. The *Ethics* are in Vol. V of *The Student's Oxford Aristotle.*

30. *Ethica Nicomachea,* 1144a4; cf. 1178a5-9.

31. *Ethica Nicomachea,* 1094a.

32. *Ibid.,* 1095a20.

33. *Ibid.,* 1095a15-30; 1098b25.

34. *Ibid.,* 1144a4. Cf. 1178a5-9.

35. *Ibid.,* 1143b7.

36. Cf. *Summa Theologica,* I, q. 6, a. 1, ad 2; *Summa Contra Gentiles,* I, 11, *Ad quartam.*

37. On this implicit desire for God in all created beings see *De Veritate,* XXII, a. 2; *In Boet. de Trinitate,* I, a. 3, ad 4.

38. I John 3, 2.

39. Cf. J.-B. Kors, O.P., *La justice primitive et le péché originel d'après s. Thomas.* Bibliothèque Thomiste, II, Le Saulchoir, 1922: "Théoriquement donc, saint Augustin ne pose pas la ques-

tion de la nature pure. Il considère seulement ce
fait, que Dieu créa l'homme dans la rectitude"
(p. 11). St. Augustine gives us his conception
of nature in the true and proper sense of the
term in *Retractationum*, I, c. 10, n. 3: ". . .
naturam, qualis sine vitio primitus condita est:
ipsa enim vere ac proprie natura hominis dicitur."
Cf. Kors, *op. cit.*, p. 10. On this whole question see the valuable note of Gilson, *Introduction
a l'étude de saint Augustin*, 2e ed., Paris, Vrin,
1943, 193, n. 1.

40.   Cf. Leahy, *op. cit.*, xiii: ". . . the man he [St.
Augustine] had in view in all his works was
precisely the man who was raised to the supernatural plane by God's grace and who was
bound for the vision of God in heaven."

41.   Cf. *De Trinitate*, XI, 6, *10;* XIII, cc. 4-6, 20,
25.

42.   *De Libero Arbitrio*, II, 9: ". . . antequam beati
simus, mentibus tamen nostris impressa est notio
beatitatis."

43.   I am aware that Rousselot denies that St.
Augustine actually made this step. Cf. "Pour
l'histoire du problème de l'amour au moyen
âge," *Beiträge zur Geschichte der Philosophie
des Mittelalters*, Band VI, Heft 6, Münster,
1908, p. 56: "Constamment saint Augustin
répète que nous désirons en tout la béatitude,
et que la béatitude ne se trouve qu'en Dieu. De
là, à affirmer qu'en tout, c'est Dieu que nous

désirons, il n'y a qu'un pas. Ce pas, il ne paraît qu'Augustin l'ait jamais fait." Among those who affirm that he did are Charles Boyer, S.J., *L'idée de vérité dans la philosophie de saint Augustin,* Paris, Beauchesne, 1940, p. 255, n. 2; Gilson, *Saint Augustin,* 140, 312; E. Portalié, "Augustin, saint," *Dictionnaire de théologie catholique,* I, 2433: "Un second principe augustinien identifie la béatitude avec Dieu lui-même;" and A. Gardeil, "Béatitude," *D.T.C.,* II, 506, n. 4. A reading of the text of St. Augustine does not seem to leave room for doubt that he identified the happiness we are seeking by a necessity of nature with God.

44. *Confessions,* X, 20, 29: "How then do I seek thee, O Lord? For when I seek thee, my God, I seek a happy life." See also *Soliloquies,* I, 2: "God, who art loved, wittingly or unwittingly, by everything that is capable of loving." In *ibid.,* n. 3, God is expressly identified with wisdom, life, beatitude, goodness, beauty, light; and creatures share in them by participating in Him.

45. *Confessions,* IV, 12, 18.

46. *Confessions,* X, 20, 29; 23, 33; 24, 35. Cf. Gilson, *Saint Augustin,* 140: "C'est Dieu que l'âme cherche sans le savoir lorsqu'elle se cherche elle-même et, par delà elle-même, la vérité béatifiante que tout homme désire." See also M. C. D'Arcy, S.J., "The Philosophy of St. Augustine," *A Monument to St. Augustine,* London, Sheed and Ward, 1934, p. 195: "And God,

Who is Truth, can He be other than the Supreme Good which all desire knowingly or unknowingly?" (the writer is paraphrasing St. Augustine).

47. *Confessions,* X, 27, *38.*

48. *De Trinitate,* VIII, 3, 4.

49. *De Trinitate,* XIV, 6, 8, 10, 12-17.

50. *De Trinitate,* XIV, 4, 6, 8, 11, 12.

51. *De Trinitate,* X, 5; XIV, 7, 8.

52. *De Trinitate,* XI, 5, 8. Cf. *ibid.,* XV, 22.

53. *De Trinitate,* IX, 12, *18.* Cf. Gilson, *Saint Augustin,* 173.

54. *Confessions,* XIII, 9, *10.* Cf. *De Civitate Dei,* XI, 28: "For the specific gravity of bodies is, as it were, their love, whether they are carried downwards by their weight, or upwards by their levity." Gilson, *Saint Augustin,* 173-4, should be read on this natural weight of the will.

55. *Saint Augustin,* 313.

56. *Soliloquies,* I, 2.

57. *De beata vita,* II, 8.

58. *De beata vita,* II, 9.

59. *De beata vita,* II, 11.

60. *De beata vita,* III, 17.

61. *De Trinitate,* XIV, 4, 6; see also IV, 3, *5.*

62. *De Civitate Dei*, XII, 1. When St. Augustine speaks of vice as an injury to nature, since it belonged to the goodness in which God created both angelic and human nature that these creatures cleave to God, he is evidently referring to the elevated state in which men and angels were created. He is not using the term *nature* in its strictly essential sense. For Baius, on the other hand, the elevated state itself (St. Augustine's *nature*) was due to human nature and natural in the essential sense. Cf. Denzinger, *Enchiridion*, n. 1026. For sin as an injury to nature in the Augustinian sense of this term see also *De Libero Arbitrio*, III, 13, 14.

63. *De Trinitate*, XIV, 12, *16*.

64. *Confessions*, I, 1, *1*.

65. *De Mysterio Trinitatis*, I, 1, *10*, S. Bonaventurae Opera Omnia, Quarrachi, 10 vols., 1892-1902, V, 46: ". . . cognitio hujus veri innata est menti rationali in q u a n t u m tenet rationem imaginis, ratione cujus insertus est sibi naturalis appetitus et notitia et memoria illius ad cujus imaginem facta est, in quem naturaliter tendit, ut in illo possit beatificari."

66. *In I Sent.*, Prolog., q. 1, n. 9: ". . . homo naturaliter appetit finem istum, quem dicit [Augustinus] supernaturalem; igitur ad istum naturaliter ordinatur; ergo ex tali ordine potest concludi iste finis ex cognitione naturae ordinatae ad ipsum. . . . Igitur naturaliter cognoscibile est

hominem ordinari secundum intellectum ad
Deum tanquam ad finem" (*Opera Omnia,* Paris,
Vivès, VIII, 20). *Ibid.,* n. 12: ". . . concedo
Deum esse finem naturalem hominis, licet non
naturaliter adipiscendum, sed supernaturaliter,
et hoc probat ratio sequens de desiderio naturali,
quam concedo" (p. 22). *In IV Sent.,* d. 49, q.
10, n. 3: "De illo appetitu naturali patet, quod
voluntas necessario et perpetuo et summe appetit
beatitudinem, et hoc in particulari" (*Opera,*
XXI, 318). *In I Sent.,* d. 48, n. 2: "Omnis
nostra volitio potissimum ordinata est ad finem
ultimum, qui est alpha et omega, principium et
finis, cui sit honor et gloria in saecula saeculorum. Amen" (*Opera,* X, 780). *In IV Sent.,*
d. 49, q. 10, n. 3: "Praeterea, illud 'appetere'
non est actus sequens cognitionem, quia tunc
esset liber; universale autem non est nisi objectum intellectus, vel consequens actum intellectus; ergo, ille appetitus non erit nisi ad
beatitudinem in particulari" (*Opera,* XXI, 318).

67. Cf. *In IV Sent.,* d. 17, q. 3, a. 1, sol. 2:
"Cuilibet rei illud est naturale quod ei a suo
creatore imponitur; tamen proprie naturalia
dicuntur quae ex principiis naturae causantur."
See also *Sum. Theol.,* III, q. 2, a. 12; q. 34, a. 3,
ad 2; q. 2, a. 1; I, q. 29, a. 2; *In II Sent.,* d. 19,
q. 1, a. 4.

68. Cf. *Con. Gent.,* IV, 19: "Unde etiam oportet
quod ex forma intelligibili consequatur in intelligente inclinatio ad proprias operationes et
proprium finem. Haec autem inclinatio in in-

tellectuali natura voluntas est." *Quaest. Disp. de Anima*, a. 13, ad 12: "Voluntas est in ratione inquantum sequitur apprehensionem rationis." *Sum. Theol.*, I-II, q. 50, a. 5, ad 3: "Voluntas ex ipsa natura potentiae inclinatur in bonum rationis." St. Thomas adopts the teaching of Aristotle that "voluntas in ratione est" (cf. *In III Sent.*, d. 27, q .2, a. 3, ad 1). *Con. Gent.*, III, 26: "Voluntas igitur, secundum quod est appetitus, non est proprium intellectualis naturae, sed solum secundum quod ab intellectu dependet." *Sum. Theol.*, I-II, q. 5, a. 8, ad 2: "Cum voluntas sequatur apprehensionem intellectus . . ." In *Sum. Theol.*, I-II, q. 6, a. 2, ad 1, the will is by definition the *appetitus rationalis.*

69. Cf. *Sum. Theol.*, I, q. 19, a. 3: "Voluntas nostra ex necessitate vult beatitudinem; sicut et quaelibet alia potentia necessariam habitudinem habet ad proprium et principale objectum."

70. *In IV Sent.*, d. 49, q. 1, a. 3, sol. 1, ad 1: "Beatitudo ergo quantum ad id quod in ipsa est per se voluntatis principale objectum, est omnibus nota; sed quantum ad id quod accidit per se objecto, non est nota." *Sum. Theol.*, I-II, q. 5, a. 8, ad 2: "Cum voluntas sequatur apprehensionem intellectus, seu rationis, . . . beatitudo ergo potest considerari sub ratione finalis boni, et perfecti, quae est communis ratio beatitudinis; et sic naturaliter, et ex necessitate voluntas in illud tendit; potest etiam considerari secundum

alias speciales considerationes, vel ex parte ipsius
operationis, vel ex parte potentiae operativae,
vel ex parte objecti: et sic non ex necessitate
voluntas tendit in ipsam." See also the *corpus* of
this article. *Sum. Theol.,* I-II, q. 13, a. 6:
"Solum autem perfectum bonum, quod est beatitudo, non potest ratio apprehendere sub ratione
mali, aut alicujus defectus; et ideo ex necessitate
beatitudinem homo vult." See also *Sum. Theol.,*
II-II, q. 17, a. 2, ad 1. Cf. *In II Sent.,* d. 38,
q. 1, a. 2, ad 2; *De Malo,* q. VI, ad 7.

71. *Sum. Theol.,* I, q. 82, a. 1, ad 2: "Voluntas,
secundum quod aliquid naturaliter vult, magis
respondet intellectui naturalium principiorum,
quam rationi, quae ad opposita se habet. Unde
secundum hoc magis est *intellectualis* quam
rationalis potestas." *In II Sent.,* d. 39, q. 2, a. 2:
"Voluntas autem rationalis, prout est natura
hominis, sive prout consequitur naturalem apprehensionem universalium principiorum juris, est
quae in bonum inclinat;" *ibid.,* ad 2: "In ratione
est aliquid naturaliter cognitum quasi principium
indemonstrabile in operabilibus, quod se habet
per modum finis. . . . Unde illud quod finis est
hominis est naturaliter in ratione cognitum esse
bonum et appetendum, et voluntas consequens
istam cognitionem dicitur voluntas ut natura."
See also *Sum. Theol.,* I, q. 83, a. 4; *De Virtutibus in Communi,* I, a. 8, ad 13; *De Malo,* q.
XVI, a. 5; *In III Sent.,* d. 17, q. 1, a. 1, sol. 3,
ad 1.

72. This is expressly asserted in *Sum. Theol.*, I-II, q. 10, a. 1; likewise in *De Verit.*, q. XXII, aa. 5 and 12.

73. *De Malo,* q. III, a. 3: "Voluntas ad nihilum ex necessitate movetur quod non apparet habere necessariam connexionem cum beatitudine, quae est naturaliter volita. . . . Bonum autem perfectum, quod est Deus, necessariam quidem connexionem habet cum beatitudine hominis, quia sine eo non potest homo esse beatus; verumtamen necessitas hujus connexionis non manifeste apparet homini in hac vita, quia Deum per essentiam non videt; et ideo etiam voluntas hominis in hac vita non ex necessitate Deo adhaereat." See also *Sum. Theol.*, I, q. 82, a. 2; *De Verit.*, q. XXVII, a. 3.

74. For Aristotle, see note 33 above. For St. Thomas, see *De Malo,* q. III, a. 3, note 73 above. Cf. *Sum. Theol.*, I, q. 82, a. 1: "Sicut intellectus ex necessitate inhaeret primis principiis, ita voluntas ex necessitate inhaeret ultimo fini, qui est beatitudo." *Ibid.,* a. 2: "Sunt enim quaedam particularia bona quae non habent necessariam connexionem ad beatitudinem, . . . et hujusmodi bonis voluntas non de necessitate inhaeret. Sunt autem quaedam h a b e n t i a necessariam connexionem ad beatitudinem, quibus scilicet homo Deo inhaeret, in quo solo vera beatitudo consistit: sed tamen, antequam per certitudinem divinae visionis necessitas hujusmodi connexionis demonstretur, voluntas non ex necessitate Deo inhaeret, nec his quae Dei sunt; sed voluntas

videntis Deum per essentiam de necessitate inhaeret Deo, sicut nunc ex necessitate volumus esse beati." See also *De Verit.*, q. XXVII, a. 3; *Sum. Theol.*, I-II, q. 10, a. 1, and ad 2; *In IV Sent.*, d. 49, q. 1, a. 3, sol. 1, ad 2: "Quamvis divina visio sit ipsa beatitudo, non tamen sequitur quod quicumque appetit beatitudinem, appetat divinam visonem; quia beatitudo, inquantum hujusmodi, importat per se objectum voluntatis, non autem ipsa divina visio; sicut aliquis appetit dulce, qui tamen non appetit mel."

75. *Sum. Theol.*, I, q. 2, a. 1, ad 1: "Cognoscere Deum esse, in aliquo communi, sub quadam confusione est nobis naturaliter insertum, inquantum scilicet Deus est hominis beatitudo; homo enim naturaliter desiderat beatitudinem; et quod naturaliter desideratur ab homine, naturaliter cognoscitur ab eodem. Sed hoc non est simpliciter cognoscere Deum esse; sicut cognoscere venientem, non est cognoscere Petrum, quamvis sit Petrus veniens; multi enim perfectum hominis bonum, quod est beatitudo, existimant divitias, quidam vero voluptates, quidam autem aliquid aliud." Cf. *Con. Gent.*, I, 11; "Sic enim homo naturaliter Deum cognoscit, sicut naturaliter ipsum desiderat. Desiderat autem ipsum homo naturaliter, in quantum desiderat naturaliter beatitudinem, quae est quaedam similitudo divinae bonitatis. Sic igitur non oportet quod Deus ipse, in se consideratus, sit naturaliter notus homini, sed similitudo ipsius."

76. *Sum. Theol.*, I, q. 2, a. 1, ad 1, in preceding note. See also *De Verit.*, q. XXII, a. 7: "Homini inditus est appetitus ultimi finis sui in communi, ut scilicet appetat naturaliter se esse completum in bonitate. Sed in quo ista completio consistat, utrum in virtutibus, vel scientiis, vel delectabilibus, vel hujusmodi aliis, non est ei determinatum a natura." This passage should be studied closely down to the end. In *Sum. Theol.*, I, q. 106, a. 2, only when God is seen by the blessed does He *sufficiently* move the will: "Nihil sufficienter movet voluntatem, nisi bonum universale, quod est Deus; et hoc bonum solus ipse ostendit, ut per essentiam videatur a beatis." See also *ibid.*, q. 82, a. 2; *De Malo*, q. III, a. 3; *ibid.*, q. V, a. 3; *ibid.*, ad 1; *In IV Sent.*, d. 49, q. 1, a. 3, sol. 1, ad 1, ad 2.

77. *Sum. Theol.*, I, q. 6, a. 1, ad 2: "Omnia, appetendo proprias perfectiones, appetunt ipsum Deum, inquantum perfectiones omnium rerum sunt quaedam similitudines divini esse." On the implicit desire for God see *De Veritate*, q. XXII, a. 2, and *Sum. Theol.*, I, q. 44, a. 4; *ibid.*, II-II, q. 34, a. 1, ad 3; *De Malo*, q. VIII, a. 2; *Con. Gent.*, II, 43; *ibid.*, III, 17, 19, 20, 24; *In II Sent.*, d. 1, q. 2, a. 2; *ibid.*, d. 37, q. 1, a. 2, ad 4.

78. *Con. Gent.*, III, 57: "Omnis intellectus naturaliter desiderat divinae substantiae visionem." *Ibid.*, III, 50: "Sicut naturale desiderium inest omnibus intellectualibus naturis ad sciendum, ita inest eis naturale desiderium ignorantiam seu

nescientiam pellendi. Substantiae autem separatae . . . cognoscunt praedicto cognitionis
modo substantiam Dei esse supra se, et supra
omne quod ab eis intelligitur, et per consequens
sciunt divinam substantiam sibi esse ignotam.
Tendit igitur naturale ipsorum desiderium ad
intelligendam divinam substantiam." *Compen-
dium Theologiae*, I, 104: "Unde semper remanet
naturale desiderium respectu perfectioris cognitionis. Impossible est autem naturale desiderium
esse vanum. . . . Non igitur naturale desiderium
sciendi potest quietari in nobis, quousque primam
causam cognoscamus, non quocumque modo, sed
per ejus essentiam." *In I Metaph.*, 1: "Quaelibet
res naturalem inclinationem habet ad suam pro-
priam operationem: . . . propria autem operatio
hominis inquantum homo, est intelligere. . . .
Unde naturaliter desiderium hominis inclinatur
ad intelligendum, et per consequens ad sciendum." *Contra Gentiles*, III, 25: "Naturaliter
inest omnibus hominibus desiderium cognoscendi
causas eorum quae videntur; unde propter ad-
mirationem eorum quae videbantur, quorum
causae latebant, homines primo philosophari
coeperunt; invenientes autem causam quiesce-
bant. Nec sistit inquisitio quousque perveniatur
ad primam causam; et tunc perfecte nos scire
arbitramur quando primam causam cognoscimus.
Desiderat igitur homo naturaliter cognoscere
primam causam quasi ultimum finem. Prima
autem omnium causa Deus est. Est igitur finis
hominis cognoscere Deum." *Con. Gent.*, III,
50: "Ex hac igitur cognitione quam habent sub-

stantiae separatae de Deo, non quiescit naturale
eorum desiderium, sed incitatur magis ad divinam substantiam videndam."

79. *Sum. Theol.*, I-II, q. 10, a. 1: "Non enim per
      voluntatem appetimus solum ea quae pertinent
      ad potentiam voluntatis, sed etiam ea quae
      pertinent ad singulas potentias, et ad totum
      hominem; unde naturaliter homo vult non solum
      objectum voluntatis sed etiam alia quae con-
      veniunt aliis potentiis; ut cognitionem veri, quae
      convenit intellectui; et esse, et vivere, et hujus-
      modi alia, quae respiciunt consistentiam natu-
      ralem; quae omnia comprehenduntur sub objecto
      voluntatis, sicut quaedam particularia bona."
      See also *De Verit.*, q. XXII, a. 5: "Quod
      voluntas de necessitate vult quasi naturali in-
      clinatione in ipsum determinata, est finis ultimus,
      ut beatitudo, et ea quae in ipso includuntur, ut
      est cognitio veritatis, et alia hujusmodi." Cf.
      ibid., a. 5; *In II Sent.*, d. 38, q. 1, a. 3, ad 4.
      In spite of this natural desire of the will to-
      wards the attainment by the other powers of their
      particular *bona* or ends, including the knowledge
      of truth by the intellect, the intellect itself, as
      well as each of our natural powers, formally
      possesses a natural desire or tendency for its
      proper object; cf. *De Anima*, a. 13, ad 11:
      "Intellectus quidem naturaliter appetit intelligibile
      ut est intelligibile; appetit enim naturaliter in-
      tellectus intelligere, et sensus sentire." In *De
      Malo*, VI, we learn that the knowledge of the
      true, which properly belongs to the intellect,

comes under the jurisdiction, so to speak, of the will to the extent that it is the *good* of the intellect to come into the possession of the true. As good, it is desired by the will; not as true. Cf. *Con. Gent.*, III, 24: ". . . nunquam enim voluntas desideraret intelligere, nisi prius intellectus ipsum intelligere apprehenderet ut bonum." Cf. *De Potentia,* q. IX, a. 9, ad 2 in contr.

80. This is the point of the teaching of *Contra Gentiles,* III, 50, where St. Thomas shows how the natural desire for knowledge present in separate substances cannot be satisfied by their natural knowledge of God: *Quod in naturali cognitione quam habent substantiae separatae de Deo non quiescit eorum desiderium.* Not even an angel, much less a human being, can reach a term that will completely satisfy his natural craving for truth and happiness, so far as his purely natural state is concerned. The mere knowledge that God exists does not completely satisfy: "Videmus autem quod videntes quia est aliquid, naturaliter scire desiderant propter quid. Ergo et cognoscentes an aliquid sit, naturaliter scire desiderant quid est ipsum; quod est intelligere ejus substantiam. Non igitur quietatur naturale sciendi desiderium in cognitione Dei qua scitur de ipso solum quia est." The whole chapter is a commentary on the unsatisfactory character of a purely natural end of man or of angel. It is unsatisfactory because it always leaves more to know of

God, and therefore more happiness to attain. A spiritual creature has no *natural* terminative end.

81. *Con. Gent.*, III, 51: "Cum autem impossibile sit naturale desiderium esse inane, quod quidem esset, si non esset possibile pervenire ad divinam substantiam intelligendam, q u o d naturaliter omnes mentes desiderant, necesse est dicere quod possibile est substantiam Dei videri per intellectum, et a substantiis intellectualibus separatis, et ab animabus nostris." That this possibility does not mean *naturally* possible is clear from the following texts: *ibid.*, 52: "Non est autem possibile quod ad istum visionis divinae modum aliqua creata substantia ex virtute propria possit attingere. . . . Videre autem Deum per ipsam essentiam divinam est proprium naturae divinae. . . . Nulla igitur intellectualis substantia potest videre Deum per ipsam divinam essentiam, nisi Deo hoc faciente." *Ibid.*: "Impossible est igitur quod aliqua substantia creata ad illam visionem perveniat, nisi per actionem divinam." *Ibid.*: "Videre autem Dei substantiam transcendit limites omnis naturae creatae; nam cujuslibet naturae intellectualis creatae proprium est, ut intelligat secundum modum suae substantiae. Substantia autem divina non potest sic intelligi, . . . Impossibile est ergo perveniri ab aliquo intellectu creato ad visionem divinae substantiae, nisi per actionem Dei, qui omnem creaturam transcendit."

82. *Con. Gent.*, II, 98: ". . . quidquid enim esse potest, intelligi potest."

83. *In IV Sent.*, d. 49, q. 2, a. 1, ad 13: "Sicut autem secundum suam naturam Deus est maxime ens; ita et secundum se est maxime intelligibilis; sed quod a nobis quandoque non intelligitur, est ex defectu nostro." Cf. *Con. Gent.*, III, 54: "Divina enim substantia non sic est extra facultatem creati intellectus, quasi aliquid omnino extraneum ab ipso. . . . Nam divina substantia est primum intelligibile, et totius intellectualis cognitionis principium. Sed est extra facultatem intellectus creati, sicut excedens virtutem ejus. . . . Indiget igitur confortari intellectus creatus aliquo divino lumine ad hoc, quod divinam essentiam videre possit."

84. The all-important text here is *Sum. Theol.*, I, q. 12, a. 4. Not even a spiritual substance such as an angel can naturally see God since its mode of being, and therefore of knowing, is not absolutely simple, as God is. This is taught in *Contra Gentiles*, III, 49 and 51.

85. *Con. Gent.*, III, 25: "Intellectus igitur, quantumcumque modicum possit de divina cognitione percipere, illud erit sibi pro ultimo fine magis quam perfecta cognitio inferiorum intelligibilium. . . . Est igitur ultimus finis hominis intelligere quoquo modo Deum."

86. *Con. Gent.*, III, 59: "Capacitas autem naturalis cujuslibet intellectus se extendit ad cognoscenda omnia genera et species, et ordinem rerum."

87. *Con. Gent.*, II, 98: "Cognoscit igitur substantia separata inferior superiorem secundum modum substantiae cognoscentis, non secundum modum substantiae cognitae, sed inferiori modo. . . . Sic igitur quaelibet substantiarum separatarum cognoscit Deum naturali cognitione secundum modum suae substantiae, per quam similes sunt Deo sicut causae." *Ibid.*, III, 52: "Videre autem Dei substantiam transcendit limites omnis naturae creatae, nam cujuslibet naturae intellectualis creatae proprium est, ut intelligat secundum modum suae substantiae. Substantia autem divina non potest sic intelligi. . . . Impossibile est ergo perveniri ab aliquo intellectu creato ad visionem divinae substantiae, nisi per actionem Dei, qui omnem creaturam transcendit."

88. *Con. Gent.*, III, 57: "Omnis intellectus naturaliter desiderat divinae substantiae visionem. Naturale autem desiderium non potest esse inane. Quilibet igitur intellectus creatus potest pervenire ad divinae substantiae visionem, non impediente inferioritate naturae." The impediment is the order of created nature itself before God as He is in himself. When the former is removed by supernatural elevation, the latter can and will be seen, but this does not make the divine substance the *natural* end or *terminus* of the created intellect. The natural desire to see God is a tendency towards an object that is not our natural end. This is possible only in the case of knowledge, where the existence of a transcendent object is known naturally while its essence can

never be naturally known. This is verified in the case of all created intelligible knowledge of God.

89. *In IV Sent.*, d. 49, q. 8, n. 6: "Omnis enim intellectus habet pro objecto totum ens, et sic non quietatur in quacumque substantia, vel ente, sed solum in ente optimo." Cf. *In I Sent.*, prolog., q. 1, n. 9: ". . . homo naturaliter appetit finem istum, quem dicit [Augustinus] supernaturalem; igitur ad istum naturaliter ordinatur; ergo ex tali ordine potest concludi iste finis ex cognitione naturae ordinatae ad ipsum. . . . Igitur naturaliter cognoscibile est hominem ordinari secundum intellectum ad Deum tanquam ad finem." *Ibid.*, n. 12: ". . . concedo Deum esse finem naturalem hominis, licet non naturaliter adipiscendum, sed supernaturaliter, et hoc probat ratio sequens de desiderio naturali, quam concedo." The first of these quotations is from vol. XXI, p. 315, of the Vivès edition of Scotus' *Opera Omnia;* the others are found in vol. VIII, pp. 20 and 22 respectively. Cf. note 66 above.

90. *In VI Sent.*, d. 49, q. 10, n. 3: "De illo naturali appetitu patet, quod voluntas necessario et perpetuo et summe appetit beatitudinem, et hoc in particulari. . . . Et quod in particulari, patet, quia appetitus est ad perfectionem intrinsecam realem, qua voluntas perficitur, sed perfectio realis non est aliquid universale, qua voluntas perficitur, sed particulari; ergo, etc." (*Opera*, XXI, 318). Cf. *In I Sent.*, d. 48, n. 2:

"Omnis nostra volitio potissimum ordinata est ad finem ultimum, qui est alpha et omega, principium et finis, cui sit honor et gloria in saecula saeculorum. Amen" (*Opera,* X, 780).

91. Cf. *In IV Sent.,* d. 49, q. 10, n. 3: "Praeterea, illud 'appetere' non est actus sequens cognitionem, quia tunc esset liber; universale autem non est nisi objectum intellectus, vel consequens actum intellectus; ergo, ille appetitus non erit nisi ad beatitudinem in particulari" (*Opera,* XXI, 318). On the purely positive reason why the essences of sensible things are the objects of the human intellect in the present state, see this important text from the *Opus Oxoniense: In I Sent.,* d. 3, q. 3, n. 24: "Si quaeritur quae est ratio istius status, respondeo, status non videtur esse nisi stabilis permanentia legibus divinae sapientiae firmata. Stabilitum est autem illis legibus sapientiae, quod intellectus noster non intelligat pro statu isto, nisi illa quorum species relucent in phantasmate, et hoc sive propter poenam originalis peccati, sive propter naturalem concordiam potentiarum animae in operando. . . . Ista tamen concordia, quae est de facto pro statu isto, non est ex natura nostri intellectus, unde intellectus est, nec etiam unde in corpore est, tunc enim in corpore glorioso necessario haberet similem concordiam, quod falsum est. Utcumque igitur sit iste status, sive ex mera voluntate Dei, sive ex mere justitia punitiva, sive ex infirmitate, quam causam Augustinus innuit, . . . saltem non est primum ob-

jectum intellectus, ut potentia est, quidditas rei materialis, sed est aliquid commune ad omnia intelligibilia, licet primum objectum adaequatum sibi in movendo pro statu isto sit quidditas rei sensibilis" (*Opera,* IX, 148). On this teaching of Duns Scotus see Cyril L. Shircel, O.F.M., *The Univocity of the Concept of Being in the Philosophy of John Duns Scotus,* Washington, 1942, especially pp. 54-55; also Patrick K. Bastable, *Desire for God,* London and Dublin, 1947, 84-99.

92. *In IV Sent., disp.* 49, q. 2, a. 1: "Homini inest appetitus naturalis ad illam veram beatitudinem quae in Dei visione consistit; non dico appetitum elicitum sed naturalem appetitum, hoc est, inclinationem naturalem et pondus naturae quo in finem illum propendet, sicut gravitas in lapide. . . ; non negamus intellectui suam inclinationem ad cognoscendum sed hominibus per voluntatem est appetere finem ultimum videre, apprehendere et possidere. . . . Potissima vero ratio quae me persuasum habet est haec. Quod homo sit imago et similitudo Dei est naturale. . . . Similitudo aut imago Dei certe non solum capacitatem dicit Dei videndi, sed naturalem et inclinationem; nam simile naturaliter appetit suum simile. . . . nulla res potest designari in quam naturalis appetitus hominis ceu in ultimum finem tendat citra illam visionem, ergo illa est noster naturalis finis in quem naturaliter ferimur."

93. J. Sestili, *De Naturali Intelligentis Animae Capacitate atque Appetitu Intuendi Divinam Essentiam,* Rome, 1896; *De Possibilitate Desiderioque Primae Causae Substantiam Videndi,* Rome, 1900. For a summary and criticism of Sestili's views, see Bastable, *Desire for God,* 71-73

94. Pierre Rousselot, S.J., *L'intellectualisme de saint Thomas,* 2 ed., Paris, Beauchesne, 1924 (English translation by Father James E. O'Mahony, O.F.M.Cap., *The Intellectualism of Saint Thomas,* New York, Sheed and Ward, 1935). For summary and criticism see Bastable, *op. cit.,* 114-117.

95. Guy de Broglie, S.J., "De la place du surnaturel dans la philosophie de saint Thomas," *Recherches de science religieuse,* 14(1924), 193-246; 481-96; 15(1925), 5-53. "Autour de la notion thomiste de la béatitude," *Archives de philosophie,* 3 (1925), 55-96. "De ultimo fine humanae vitae asserta quaedam," *Gregorianum,* 9 (1928), 628-30. "Du charactère mystérieux de notre élévation surnaturel," *Nouvelle revue théologique,* 64 (1937), 337-76. Cf. Bastable, 117-9.

96. Joseph Maréchal, S.J., *Le point de départ de la métaphysique,* cahier V, Louvain, 1926, p. 315: "Nous conclurons avec S. Thomas que l'impulsion naturelle de nos facultés intellectives les oriente vers l'intuition immédiate de l'Être absolu; que cette intuition, à vrai dire, dépasse la puis-

sance et excède l'exigence de toute intelligence
finie livrée à ses seules ressources naturelles . . ."
See Bastable, 119-20, for summary and criticism.

97.   A. Laporta, O.S.B., "Les notions d'appétit
naturel et de puissance obédientielle chez saint
Thomas d'Aquin," *Ephemerides Theologicae
Lovanienses,* 5 (1928), 257-77. Cf. p. 257:
"Par appétit naturel de la vision béatifique les
commentateurs modernes de saint Thomas en-
tendent généralement un désir élicite, un désir
qui est libre même, puisque 'conditionné, im-
parfait, pure velléité.' Saint Thomas, il faut bien
le reconnaître, parle d'autre chose. Pour lui
appetitus naturalis désigne un appétit défini par
la nature même, nécessaire donc et tout à l'opposé
d'une aspiration libre. . . . il est question chez lui
non pas du vouloir naturel qui est un acte, mais
d'une pure ordination transcendental de finalité,
du pondus naturae comme a si bien dit Soto.
Tout en affirmant qu'il existe, dans toute créature
intelligente, une tendance ontologique à la béatitude surnaturelle, saint Thomas nie que celle-ci
constitue l'objet de l'appétit naturel élicite de
leur volonté." See Bastable, 120-1.

98.   James E. O'Mahony, O.F.M.Cap., *The Desire
of God in the Philosophy of St. Thomas Aquinas,*
Cork University Press, 1929. Cf. p. 252: "Nothing, therefore, could be clearer than the meaning of 'natural desire' as signifying the transcendental relation of a particular nature to its end
or perfection." P. 174: "For St. Thomas beati-

tude which would be final, must bring with it
the appeasing of the creature's 'natural desire.'
And natural desire for him is the inherent tendency of the creature towards its ultimate perfection. It follows that natural perfection is not
the term of the creature's natural desire. . . .
Natural beatitude is only possible because nature
tends beyond it, in its desire of ultimate perfection, in its desire of God." The "beatific
vision" is the term of this natural desire (pp.
140, 194). For Bastable's summary and analysis
of O'Mahony's views see *op. cit.*, 121-132.

99.   Henri de Lubac, S.J., *Surnaturel,* Paris, Aubier,
      1946.

100.   *Surnaturel,* 109: "On le voit, . . . Dominique
      Soto ne rompt encore avec la position essentielle
      de saint Augustin et de saint Thomas—comme
      de saint Bonaventure et de Duns Scot—qui
      n'avaient jamais envisagé comme possible pour
      l'homme ou pour quelque esprit que ce fût, une
      fin à la fois transcendante et naturelle, consistant
      dans une autre connaissance de Dieu que la
      vision béatifique." *Ibid.,* 121: "Scot, en effet,
      proclamait tout comme saint Thomas, en des
      termes peut-être plus frappants mais dans une
      conviction identique, que l'inadéquation foncière
      qui existe entre la fin de la créature spirituelle
      et les moyens naturels dont elle dispose pour y
      atteindre, était la marque propre de sa dignité.
      . . . En plein XVIᵉ siécle, Dominique de Soto
      demeure fidèle à la tradition, soucieux une fois
      de plus de recueillir en sa doctrine les grandes

idées que saint Thomas et Duns Scot avaient
également tenues, qui n'étaient spécifiquement
ni thomistes ni scotistes mais simplement chré-
tiennes."

101.   The conclusion of *Surnaturel,* entitled "Exigence divine et désir naturel," is important as a
concise resume of de Lubac's views. Cf. p. 486:
"S'il y a dans notre nature un désir de voir
Dieu, ce ne peut être que parce que Dieu veut
pour nous cette fin surnaturelle qui consiste à le
voir. C'est parce que, la voulant et ne cessant
de la vouloir, il en dépose et ne cesse d'en
déposer le désir dans notre nature. En sorte que
ce désir n'est autre que son appel." P. 487:
"Le monstre de l'exigence n'était donc qu'un
fantôme. . . . Si ce désir exige, au sens que
nous avons dit, d'être comblé, c'est que déjà
Dieu même est à sa source, bien qu'encore
'anonyme.' Désir naturel du surnaturel: c'est en
nous l'action permanente du Dieu qui crée notre
nature, comme la grâce est en nous l'action
permanente du Dieu qui crée l'ordre moral."
Father de Lubac seems to have "exorcised the
monster of 'exigence'" (p. 486) by simply
transferring it from the creature to the creator.
Is not this postponing the difficulty instead of
answering it? Does it not raise more and
deeper problems than it settles?

102.   *Con. Gent.,* III, 25: "Cujuslibet effectus cog-
niti naturaliter homo causam scire desiderat. Intellectus autem humanus cognoscit ens universale.

Desiderat igitur naturaliter cognoscere causam ejus, quae solum Deus est." *Ibid.,* 112: "Unaquaeque intellectualis substantia est quodammodo omnia, inquantum totius entis comprehensiva est suo intellectu . . ."

103. The need of the *lumen gloriae* is not absolute for Duns Scotus but only hypothetical and conditional. If in the beatific vision the created intellect elicits an operation, then it is required to take the place of created species. If, however, the intellect is merely passive in this vision, the *lumen gloriae* is not required. Cf. *In IV Sent.,* d. 49, q. 11, n. 10: ". . . si autem intellectus sit mere passivus, . . . tunc non requiritur lumen gloriae" (*Opera,* XXI, 418). See also *In III Sent.,* d. 14, q. 2, nn. 2, 3, 5, 8 (*Opera,* XIV, 492-501).

104. Cf. *Con. Gent.,* II, 97: "Cognoscit igitur substantia separata inferior superiorem, secundum modum substantiae cognoscentis, non secundum modum substantiae cognitae, sed inferiori modo; superior autem inferiorem eminentiori modo. . . . Quaelibet substantiarum separatarum cognoscit Deum naturali cognitione secundum modum suae substantiae, per quam similes sunt Deo sicut causae." While it is true, therefore, that being is the proper object of the intellect, yet, since knowledge takes place after the manner of a likeness and only the infinite being, God, has, as it were, in Himself a likeness of all being precisely because He is not determined to

any species or genus of being, God alone in His essence knows all being. Every other intelligible nature is determined to some genus and species of being, which defines the range of its natural knowledge. The paragraph beginning "Hoc autem sic" is important on this point. It is necessary to bear in mind this natural ordination of man to a knowledge of separate, immaterial substances in the next life. This is all St. Thomas is speaking about in the passage Father de Lubac cites on p. 120 of *Surnaturel.* A reference to the objection as well as to the reply (*In Boet. de Trin.,* q. 6, a. 4, ad 5 [*not* ad 15m]) will show that the beatific vision is not in question at all.

105.　See note 80 above.

106.　Cf. *Con. Gent.,* III, 44: "Opinio Aristotelis fuit quod ultima felicitas, quam homo in vita ista acquirere potest, sit cognitio de rebus divinis qualis per scientias speculativas haberi potest." *Ibid.,* 48: "Quia vero Aristoteles vidit quod non est alia cognitio hominis in hac vita, quam per scientias speculativas, posuit hominem non consequi felicitatem perfectam, sed suo modo. In quo satis apparet, quantam angustiam patiebantur hinc inde eorum praeclara ingenia, a quibus angustiis liberabimur, si ponamus . . . hominem ad veram felicitatem post hanc vitam pervenire posse, anima hominis immortali existente. . . . Erit igitur ultima felicitas hominis in cognitione Dei, quam habet humana mens post hanc vitam per modum quo ipsum cognoscunt substantiae separatae." *Sum. Theol.,* I, q. 62, a. 1: "Unde et Aristoteles perfectissimam hominis contemplationem, qua optimum intelligible, quod est Deus, contemplari potest in hac vita, dicit esse ultimam hominis felicitatem: sed super hanc felicitatem est alia felicitas, quam in futuro expectamus, qua videbimus Deum sicuti est."

107. St. Thomas clearly teaches the non-terminative character of the natural end of man in *In Boet. de Trin.,* q. II, a. 1, ad 7: "Cum Deus in infinitum a creatura distet, nulla creatura movetur in Deum ut ipsi adaequetur, vel recipiendo ab ipso, vel cognoscendo ipsum. Hoc igitur quod creatura in infinitum distat, non est terminus motus creaturae; sed quaelibet creatura movetur ad hoc quod Deo assimiletur plus et plus quantum potest: et sic etiam humana mens debet semper moveri ad cognoscendum de Deo plus et plus secundum modum suum. Unde dicit Hilarius: 'Qui pie infinita persequitur, etsi non contingat aliquando, tamen proficiet prodeundo." See also *Con. Gent.,* III, 49, 50.

108. *Scholastica Commentaria in Primam Partem Angelici Doctoris d. Thomae,* Rome, 1584, q. 12, a. 1; col. 237: "Divus Thomas non vult demonstrare quod in homine sit naturale desiderium videndi Deum; sed proposita fide, quae dicit visionem beatificam esse possibilem, ostendit illud esse maxime consentaneum intellectui

creato. . . . In creatura spirituali est quaedam
velleitas et quoddam desiderium imperfectum
videndi Deum. Ex quo colligit D. Thomas
probabiliter quod visio beatifica sit possibilis, ne
frustretur tale desiderium naturale."

109. *In Summam Theologicam,* I-II, q. 3, ad 8
(Leonine edition of the *Sum. Theol.,* VI, 36):
"Desiderium namque potest dici naturale a
natura ut subjecto tantum: et sic naturaliter
desideramus visionem Dei. . . . Posset quoque
dici quod Auctor tractat de homine ut theologus
. . . Et sic, licet homini absolute non insit naturale
hujusmodi desiderium, est tamen naturale homini
ordinato a divina providentia in illam patriam."
Bastable lists Cajetan's natural desire for God
under the heading of a freely elicited act, free
both in regard to its specification and in regard
to its exercise (*op. cit.,* 83, 112). This, however, is by no means certain. In his commentary on the *Sum. Theol.,* I, q. 78, a. 1, Cajetan
speaks of the innate natural desire that is not an
elicited act and of the elicited natural desire that
is an act determined by nature, examples of
which latter are the natural desire to know, to
live, to be, and for beatitude. For Brisbois (E.
Brisbois, S.J., "Le désir de voir Dieu et la
métaphysique du vouloir selon saint Thomas,"
Nouvelle revue théologique, 63 (1936), p. 983)
Cajetan, unlike Bañez, gives to the texts of St.
Thomas which speak of a natural desire for God
the proper sense of "natural" as denoting complete finality and exigence of its object: he does

not mean only non-repugnance or obediential potency. The only restriction he places on this natural desire is that it is hypothetical: it does not come into being except on the hypothesis of supernatural elevation. This elevation awakens in a man a natural desire to know all that the human mind can know. In fact, however, Cajetan was so puzzled by St. Thomas' natural desire for God that he never quite knew what to make of it. He gives more than one explanation of it, and the explanations he gives are more of the nature of possible solutions than definitive statements.

110. *In Contra Gentiles*, III, 51 (Leonine edition of the *Contra Gentiles*, XIV, 141): "Et in proposito naturale desiderium videndi divinam essentiam est actus voluntatis de necessitate consequens quantum ad specificationem actus illam cognitionem qua cognoscitur per effectus *quia est* de Deo." Cf. *ibid.*, I, 5 (Leonine, XIII, 16): "Sanctus Thomas autem per naturalem inclinationem intelligit non inclinationem naturae oppositam inclinationi quae sequitur cognitionem, sed actum elicitum a voluntate qui est naturalis et determinatus quantum ad specificationem actus, non autem quantum ad exercitium."

111. St. Thomas' doctrine of freedom of specification and of exercise may be seen in *De Malo*, q. V; *De Verit.*, q. XXII, a. 6; and in *Sum. Theol.*, I, q. 82, a. 2. Sylvester of Ferrara explains this doctrine correctly: "Et est sensus

verborum ejus quod, si proponatur voluntati ultimus finis et beatitudo in communi, voluntas quidem potest elicere et non elicere actum circa illud objectum, sed si eliciat actum circa illud, ille actus erit prosecutio, et non potest voluntas tale objectum refugere, licet homo non possit ad illud bonum propria virtute pervenire" (*In Con. Gent.*, I, 5, Leonine, XIII, 16). So far he refers to happiness in general. In what follows he seems to assume that St. Thomas applies this doctrine to the desire for the beatific vision as something that can be proposed to the will as good from every point of view: "Non est autem inconveniens quod homo in aliquid inclinetur per actum voluntatis naturalem modo dicto, et tamen illud non possit propria virtute adipisci: quia licet ad illud virtus naturalis non sufficiat, proponitur tamen voluntati sub ratione appetibilis ex omni parte et nullum habentis boni defectum, ex quo habet voluntas ut non possit illud respuere." It is, we have seen, the teaching of St. Thomas that no object, not even God as He appears to us in this world, is seen as good from every point of view. In thinking that God can be so represented to the will Sylvester unwittingly puts himself in the middle of the Augustinian-Scotistic stream.

112.   See note 73 above.

THE AQUINAS LECTURES

Published by the Marquette University Press,
Milwaukee 3, Wisconsin

The Nature and Origins of Scientism (1944) by Fr. John Wellmuth, S.J., Chairman of the Department of Philosophy, Xavier University.

Cicero in the Courtroom of St. Thomas Aquinas (1945) by the late E. K. Rand, Ph.D., Litt.D., LL.D., Pope Professor of Latin, *emeritus*, Harvard University.

St. Thomas and Epistemology (1946) by Fr. Louis-Marie Régis, O.P., Th. L., Ph. D., director of the Albert the Great Institute of Mediaeval Studies, University of Montreal.

St. Thomas and the Greek Moralists (1947, Spring) by Vernon J. Bourke, Ph. D., professor of philosophy, St. Louis University, St. Louis, Missouri.

History of Philosophy and Philosophical Education (1947, Fall) by Étienne Gilson of the Académie française, director of studies and professor of the history of mediaeval philosophy, Pontifical Institute of Mediaeval Studies, Toronto.

The Natural Desire for God (1948) by Fr. William R. O'Connor, S.T.L., Ph. D., professor of dogmatic theology, St. Joseph's Seminary, Dunwoodie, N.Y.

First in Series (1937) $1.00; all others $1.50

Uniform format, cover and binding.